PENGUIN MODE[...]

The Penguin Modern Po[...]
diversity of contempora[...]
representative selections from the work of three poets now writing,
allowing the curious reader and the seasoned lover of poetry to
encounter the most exciting voices of our moment.

MALIKA BOOKER is a British writer of Guyanese and Grenadian parentage. Her pamphlet *Breadfruit* was published by flipped eye in 2007, and her first collection, *Pepper Seed*, published in 2013 by Peepal Tree, was shortlisted for the Seamus Heaney Centre for Poetry Prize. She has written for the stage and radio, and was the first Poet in Residence at the Royal Shakespeare Company. She is currently a Douglas Caster Fellow at the University of Leeds.

SHARON OLDS was born in San Francisco. She was the New York State Poet Laureate from 1998 to 2000 and currently teaches at New York University. She has been involved with outreach writing workshops at hospitals for the physically challenged and for veterans of the Iraq and Afghanistan wars. Her collection *Stag's Leap* won the T. S. Eliot Prize and the 2013 Pulitzer Prize; her latest, *Odes*, was published by Cape Poetry in 2016.

WARSAN SHIRE is a Somali-British poet. Her pamphlets are *Teaching My Mother How to Give Birth* (2011) and *Her Blue Body* (2015). In 2013 she won the first Brunel University African Poetry Prize. She was made the inaugural Young Poet Laureate for London in 2014 and served as Poet in Residence for Queensland, Australia, in 2014. In 2016 she collaborated with Beyoncé Knowles Carter on the film adaptation and poetry of the visual album *Lemonade*. Her work has been translated into several languages. Her debut collection is forthcoming from flipped eye publishing.

MODERN POETS 3

Your Family, Your Body

Malika Booker

Sharon Olds

Warsan Shire

PENGUIN BOOKS

PENGUIN BOOKS

UK | USA | Canada | Ireland | Australia
India | New Zealand | South Africa

Penguin Books is part of the Penguin Random House group of companies
whose addresses can be found at global.penguinrandomhouse.com

This collection first published 2017
005

Poems by Malika Booker copyright © 2007, 2013, 2017
Poems by Sharon Olds copyright © 2005, 2009, 2012, 2016
Poems by Warsan Shire copyright © 2011, 2015, 2017

The moral right of the authors has been asserted

Set in Warnock Pro 9.65/12.75 pt
Typeset by Jouve (UK), Milton Keynes
Printed and bound in Great Britain by Clays Ltd, Elcograf S.p.A.

A CIP catalogue record for this book is available from the British Library

ISBN: 978-0-141-98401-8

www.greenpenguin.co.uk

CONTENTS

MALIKA BOOKER

WARSAN SHIRE

Malika Booker

Red Ants Bite

1

You will be a whore just like your mother
Granny told me all the time,
like saying good morning.

I tried to make her love me,
but her mouth was brutal,
like hard-wire brush, it scraped me,

took skin off my bones, made me bleed
where no one could see,
so I'd shrink, a tiny rocking foetus.

You will end up on your back, scunt spread out,
feet sprawl out, whoring. Who tells a child that?
Yet I loved her. She was my granny,

and I wanted her to love me back,
but every day her words
put this hard thing deep inside me.

2

I wanted her to give me juicy mangoes and kisses,
I wanted pepperpot and tennis rolls;
she gave me rocks and hard stone,

pelted me each day, and I loved her still.
I told my doll that too much coconut oil
in Granny's hair rancid her mouth.

MALIKA BOOKER   3

I am grown and the smell of mothballs
curdles my stomach. I wanted mangoes and kisses:
You will be a whore just like your mother.

My father was her everything,
my brother her world.
Her daughters reaped zigar.

3

Her mouth spat, *You black ugly scunt.*
I was her black thick molasses, dunce and sour,
her burnt cassava. I was pone charred in the oven,
I was strong bitters, a brew better off unborn.

And I still wished her eyes could swallow me whole
the way they did my brother Philip. He would hug me
to transfer Granny's glow to my world and I love him still.

Even when baby Kwesi came along, she never let go
of her apple-eye, but he never let go of us.

4

Yes! You red-skin, mixed-blood, nigger woman,
young, you were gold in Guyana's sun,
your face a dark cream to my bitter chocolate,
eyes hazel like mine. We are kin, you and I.
Your blood pumps through me. How could you
scratch me so deep, leaving lacerations?

Yes, Jesse, tell me what hardened your heart
to your son's first-born girl-child? Tell me,
Granny, now you dead, buried
in that Buxton graveyard, do you cuss me still?

Remember when Mummy went away
you came to stay at our house:
how I was your shadow; how I followed you,
wanting to fix the wrong you saw in me.
Your cruel tongue banished me to slide down
my wall in the corner crying, *Oh meh Goy, why?
Granny, what I do to you, eh?*

5

It was the house over by the Buxton train line,
the house with the wooden front steps
and the old white rocking chair, those stairs
where you followed Mum, heaping curses
like red ants' bites, spewing *Rasshole, scunt, whore.*

Your son had outside women? So what!
Mum ran ashamed; necks craned from windows
as you peppered her skin with cuss,
till she flogged a taxi on the highway.

Years later Mum tells me the story
after I ask her to go back to Guyana with me.
The entire plane journey Mum mutters, *Wicked woman.*
We walk up those same wooden stairs,
the divorced wife, the scarred granddaughter.

At ninety-six you could claim fifty years,
that day I saw you sit in the rocking chair,
saw my mother part your hair, pour coconut oil,
massage, then plait, her fingers caressing strands.

It's water under the bridge, she tells me later.
I can't talk past the words buried deep,

can't talk past the men I froze beneath,
your words branded under the skin
inside my thighs, legs spread like a whore.

Oh mother, humbled I watch you
plait the hair of an old woman
I wanted to love me years ago.

6

Jesus look where you brought me from,
I was down in the world doing what I please
But look where you bought me from . . .

He had me one and let me go,
I don't know why Satan let me go . . .
Caribbean Gospel – Jump for Jesus.

I lived till me turn one hundred and one,
live through back-break in backra sun.
I was a slave baby mixed with plantation white.
This creamy skin draw buckman, blackman,

coolieman, like prize. And if you did hear sweet talk,
if you did see how much fine fuck I get.
Is hard life, hard, hard life and only one son I bear.
My mother tell me to kill di girl child dem –

they only bring hard ears. *Jessie, harden you heart*
to them girl. But I tell you, Miss, I never kill no child,
and is one boychild I breed, only one, then pure girls.
I didn't right to vex?

I was the lone woman every man want to advantage,
I had was to sharpen meh mouth like razor blade,
turn red in seconds till bad word spill blood.
Scunt-hole child, you want sorry?

Jessie Spenser never tell a soul sorry when she live,
you sure not getting one now me dead.
Wait for that and you go turn dust.
And what I ever do you, Missy?

I ever fire licks like rain scatter on ground
in rainy season pon you skin? No.
I tell you nuff ole higue story on back stairs.
I toughen you soffie-ness, mek man can't fuck you
easy so. So fuck off, leave the dead some peace.

Pepper Sauce

I pray for that grandmother, grinding her teeth,
one hand pushing in fresh hot peppers, seeds and all, turning
the handle of that old iron mill, squeezing the limes, knowing
      they will burn and cut raw like acid.
She pours in vinegar and gets Anne to chop five onions
      with a whole bulb of garlic,
      Chop them up real fine girl, you hear?
And Anne dicing, and crying, relieved that no belt has
                                blistered her skin,
      no knife handle smashed down onto her knuckles
until they bleed for stealing money from she grandmother
                                     purse.

I hear she made Anne pour in the oil and vinegar
      and stir up that hot sauce, how she hold her down.
I hear she tied that girl to the bedposts,
      strung her out naked, like she there lying on a crucifix.
I hear she spread she out, then say,
      I go teach you to go and steal from me, Miss Lady.
I hear she scoop that pepper sauce out of a white enamel bowl,
      and pack it deep into she granddaughter's pussy,
I hear there was one piece of screaming in the house that day.
      Anne bawl till she turn hoarse,
            bawl till the hair on the neighbour's skin raise up,
            bawl till she start hiss through her teeth,
            bawl till she mouth could make no more sound,
I hear how she turn raw,
how that grandmother leave her there all day,

I hear how she couldn't walk or talk for weeks.

Saltfish

My mother wanted to boil the salt out of the fish,
so much harsh salt, then chip that saltfish smaller
and smaller, so she could cope with the hawked spit
of her patients, their hatred gutting her raw
so that some days she wanted to tell them,
It's only skin, we bleed the same underneath,
but she held it in. Some days she wanted to crawl
back into her mother's belly, her little island home
and be safe. Some days she wished she had stayed
in that small place because if you study the damn dogs
in this place, they go bite you up, break you down.
Every day you feel like your teeth cracking on hard
stale cassava bread. This place ain't winning at all;
is like they don't realise we can still go back home.

Exodus

She does not talk about that time.
She has buried it deep in the earth
where you bury shit.
Buried it with no wake,
no funeral, no coffin, no fanfare,
buried it whilst it was raw, stink and bitter.
It was early September. The phone ring.
Jerk out of sleep. Fumble. The red sky
of pre-dawn through my bare window.
My cousin's Guyanese tones, low,
whispering, voice broken. She sobs,
till I, too, begin to cry.

She stutters, stops, starts, tells me
about an advert, a plane ride.
They promised her work and a US visa.
I am a prisoner somewhere
in the South; they take my passport,
work us long hours, deduct our pay
for food and board, then give us a trickle.
I made more back home. We pick fruit all day.

She left her girlchild home in her mother's care,
now can't send them no money.
I can't see me way . . . help me, she sobs.
I make phone calls to older aunts in New York,
not new to this, who tell me they will take care of it.
A month later they call to say, *We have her.*
How? I ask. But they have buried it, too.
We do not talk about them things.

The Overseer's Lament

1

The overseer dead and he whip sprout
scarlet lilies. Whole cane fields bowed,
yea who wield whip with skill dead,
he who hit them roped bodies wearing blindfold,
he who lash don't miss, dead.

He who sing, *this job is too sweet*, as he fleck,
bloody raindrops from blistering skin gone
causing women to raise up they red petticoats
and dance, trampling he gravesite

while mosquitoes refuse to suck blood
and fireflies lose their light.

2

He death suck earth dry: weeds run riot
in burial ground, cat whips sprout scarlet lilies,
machetes pound stone, lips drown rum,
and home made spirit.

He disappeared from their thoughts
in a finger click. That was one piece of no funeral
where Angie wrap that long skirt tight
so she could sway to leaves clapping
on the trees where she used to hang and swing
licks raining on her skin like scattered rice.
Oh the splek and splak of that rope!

Now she prays to Gods to pelt him
with hard rock, to peel he skin

from he bones, make he crawl like swine.
This day when the mosquitoes strike
and the fireflies cease to glow.

3

Wickedness crumble he body to dust in a finger click.
Who beat drum and chant themselves into a trance.
Who plant flower seed with light heart. Who talk
to Jumbie, begging them to whip he hard down there,
beat he with bamboo, make he body bear red hibiscus,
he face turn ripe tomato, make his seed dry and burn.

Oh now he dead life sweet like ripe cane
and children's laughter fresh like spring water.

Warning

1

Some great-grandmother told her daughter,
Never let no man hit you and sleep,
pepper the food, boil hot water and throw,
use knife and make clean cut down there,
use cutlass and chop, then go police.
Each daughter told over and over,
like *brush your teeth*, till it stick.
How my mother run-way man with cutlass,
chase him. How my gran use cutlass pon table
to explain to her man, *Don't lose your blasted mind*
and raise that hand on me.
And so we are shaped, moulded and made hard.
I remember my aunt kicked her man out
after her child was born, cut him dead
like rotten wood, after he use her like boxing bag,
kicking her womb as she lay on the floor.
That day her blood boiled through swell eye
and buss skin. She knew he could not sleep; he knew
she wanted to kill him bad bad, chop him dead . . .

2

Raised in London soil and Guyana sun,
I never understood that need for cutlass,
where it came from, till I visited Grenada,
a place where man fist pound woman flesh
like kneading hard dough. I see bull strength
knock girls flat out when she man full of rum
and carnival. How Ronald buss lash in he woman ass
every Friday and Saturday night, kick she down,
buss she tail. And next day is black eye and bruise.

As Pauline clings onto Ronald's foot, saying
she love him through each blow, I understand.

    3

I never knew I had it. Thought I was soft,
till that night my friend could not drive
and I offered him my bed to sleep.
I felt something in his look, he and I
alone in that room, and my blood raised up.
My pores swelled, I went to the kitchen,
took down that knife, marched upstairs,
told him, *I cutting it off if you lose your mind.*
Don't think it. And if you do, don't sleep.

Cement

Last week my tears were sucked out
with our aborted child. Yesterday
in the shower, pain contorted me;
I squatted, expelled a souvenir:

red, liver-textured, squeezed out.
I scooped it up and flushed it away.
You were not there. Your absence
no longer makes me cry.

My tears are gone, so I plaster my heart
against every grit-worried wound.
Now I understand older black women
like my aunts, their hard posture,

why I never saw them cry.
My father made my mother stony,
a martyr for her kids, brittle and bitter,
till my stepdad unbricked her wall;

layer by layer I watched it crumble.
My aunt, shattered by fists, blocked her heart;
stone cold, her tears dried up.
All my life, I never saw her cry, until, foetal

in a hospital bed, wrapped in my mother's arms,
facing death, tears tracking her face,
she whispered, *I am scared.*
Crying for all her tear-barren years.

Washing water-diluted blood down the drain,
bleaching the bath tiles white, I want to bawl
my eyes out, but I have learnt my lesson well.
Each passing day hardens my voice.

Erasure

This is no elegy; no one can write elegies
for such as you. There are no scuff marks here
for your erasure. No etches on a strong barked tree.

There was no grief. You are my silence.
Why do you choose to rise now like shifting sand
blown by a slight breeze?

You were my simple crime against humanity,
and, like a criminal, I claim no regrets.
I buried you too deep to call you a name;

you are my trail of invisible lines
like the stretch marks that did not have time to form.
No guilt resides in my house.

I did what we women have always done.
I froze the tears into a block of ice
buried so deep that the guilt is a cold in me,

a thing that will not melt.
What can I say to you who never breathed, you callous dust?
I can talk of sacrifices, broken lives.

I can talk of Abraham almost cutting Isaac's throat.
But this was no holy decision.
I cannot tell you why I said no to you.

I am a worn white dress, all ash and grey.
Unspeakable requiem, do not rise now.
Do not ask me the worth.

Waiting for Father

Little kernels of corn explode. My mother's nose sweats,
her calm spirals into a scarlet cyclone,
those nights we popped and buttered popcorn,

then sat waiting for my father,
waiting to stick ourselves to those leather seats
in his grey Cortina, clip speakers to the windows,

and eat popcorn at the drive-in movie.
His arrival depended on the law of averages,
and statistics strongly supported non-arrival.

Evenings we sat believing it would be different.
How could he not come? He was a kite,
dancing in our clouds. How could we not see

that we clenched the fraying thread of a high flyer;
a flamboyant cockerel parading in sunshine with his floozies.
Ah Fatthaa! How could you? How could you?

Sweet Liquor

'Left right, left right in the Government boots
The Government boots
I see them boots, boots, boots and more boots
On the feet of young trigger-happy recruits'
    – *The Mighty Gabby*

girl, if you see thing! the way they does pile in here when fete
door bus open on saturday nights. pour in like animals. looking
sweet too bad. girl, if you see the way they does parade and carry
on. how i does close meh eyes and lean back on them hard bodies
and wine. i know some of them real good. the way they move.
how they handle women bodies. the way they does roll they hip.
girl, you have to know them tings, so when a man come jam
behind you, you could know if is friend or foe without turning
round and looking up in he face. or in case the place too dark to
make out they face. you know if to walk off or stay there. girl, i
know they faces real good but never look in they eyes.

if you does see the way they hold on to rum bottles like is
    communion.
like is holy. like is they saviour. the way they does crawl
all up inside hard liquor. girl, if you see them wring out johnny
walker bottle. squeeze every drop. knock back wray and nephew
just like real beast riding they soul.

girl, to see sweet young ting hurt so bad does make pain buss meh
belly. when they play that fay-ann song that say, *everybody*
    everybody
bounce somebody, bounce somebody, girl, if you see ting! a host of
unruly joy. them man does tek over the dancefloor and smash
they bodies, flesh hitting flesh, jumping and hollering like the
army evict them, like them bodies have nuff sin to wuk out they

system. last night ashley tell me he name call and he going over there soon. girl, and when he tell me dat, i mek the mistake of looking he in he eyes. if you see them eyes! i frighten men with eyes dead so. like all the love wring out of them. i does wonder what the hell them see so, make sadness line they eyes like cataract. oh lord, girl, what I see in he eyes mek meh own eye spring water. he so young, baby still in he chin and he standing there body lean to one side, squeezing the bottle neck, choking it nah backfoot! girl, what I could say eh! stupid tie up meh tongue, so I jus do hold onto him all night, sweet he up with meh body, and pile he ass with more liquor.

After Liming in the Local Rum Shop on Diamond Street,

he slashed his cutlass across her face,
her raised hand failed to shield

against the second blow.
One finger cut clean off.

She deserved it, Auntie Julie said.
I know, if it was her daughter,

she would hunt and gut him
like wild manicou.

Reggae blares from Eggie's rum shop,
Miss Junes practises hymns for the church choir.

This street is a child's playground
where all the sounds battle until they harmonise.

But there's no fight here. Well,
two little girls punch up, stop talk, then make up.

They say *Is not he fault, too much Clarke's Court
full he belly and heat up he blood.*

She took him back in.
I hear no apology left his lips.

Vigil

1

Her youngest daughter searches
for a funeral dress and white veil.
Her eldest daughter folds in;
her son disappears into heroin.

I ask only that my aunt wait for me,
the way her mother waited for her,
holding death back with laboured breath,
eyes fixed ahead, living

to see her daughter that last time.
I ask her to wait so I can watch
her steady fingers turn the rosary beads,
kiss the baby hair by her ear,

smile when she tells me she is scared.
I don't want her to be alone.
I am confident, like God,
packing for my early morning flight.

At 3 am the phone rings. She's gone.
There is a still pause before I weep.

2

Today I walk along the River Thames
following a procession,
nostalgic as the season dies,

watching rust-coloured leaves litter
as Indian gods, samba dancers,
and fish lanterns glide in the night.

Last year I walked in this sea of bodies,
saying poems about crossroads
to veil-faced Orishas, lifeless puppets.

I walked dressed in white
like her face covered in that coffin.
I walked preparing for my vigil,

ticking off hours to my flight.
It's a year today.
I knew she would wait,

but she slipped out real quiet
and gone she own way.

Burial Ground

There are dark places drunk with grief where water
drizzles. There are wilted flowers and dried wreaths.
There is your grave hidden back there, behind
God's back. There are clusters of Charles
buried here, neighbours in this family plot.
Two lone wooden stumps mark the grave
where you wait for that marble headstone
etched with your name. There is wild bush
and the broken fence where your nephew
crashed that rented car at your funeral,
when his vision blurred with tears. There are
the marks we leave and those that will be made.

Faith

1

The museum is an empty house, a dead lifestyle.
In the living room, pictures of Jesus forlorn,
an old rosary hanging over the bed.
This how we lived in old days, they tell me.
I understand old ones die, like you did, Aunty,
the way your soul left your body, blank
on bleached sheets, the way these people
left their home. I look at this old bed now;
did a mother die here, choking on her spit too?
Is this her rosary? Did she lose it all?

I visit the hospital a month before you die,
your left big toe is a blackening cherry.
Cut it, we beg, but our pleas are moot;
you are Taurus. Stoic. Resolute.

The day you lose your rosary for two days,
we search under beds and in fruit bowls.
You cry nonstop all night. Nurses sift mountains
of soiled sheets until the rosary is found nestled
in your dirty pillow case. When they give it to you,

your fingers continue rolling as if it had not strayed.
Then you, who clutched your faith like a second skin,
whisper to me, *I have lost faith in my Lord.*

2

I want to write a hymn for you
where voices lift and southern Black choirs rock.

I want to write a hymn for you
where the sinners writhe, weeping bitter tears.

I want to write a hymn for you
where Baptist priests fling words at the congregation like fire
and Catholic priests throw holy water into the sky.

I want to write a classic hymn all harps and harmonicas,
a hymn where our slave grandmas lift up their long frocks
and trample the earth to sounds of tambourines.

I want to write calypso hymns, folk hymns,
reggae hymns, joyous hymns.
I want to write sweet hymns for you.

Libation

Slovenia, 2008

It is the Night of the Dead, the graveyards are packed
as relatives lay flowers, light flames, talk to their dead.
It is beautiful: the flowers, the moon, and silence.
I am in Kocevje, my relatives buried so far away.
I do not honour anyone. I am ugly here.

How could I forsake my own dead?
Aunty, each year you placed white candles
and holy water in every doorway of our home
for our departed, then we prayed over food
left on plates with glasses of water to feed our dead.

Now no Jesus pictures hang on my wall,
No 'God bless this house' sign on my door.
Yes, I write poems for you, but that is not enough;
I have forgotten our ways and am ashamed.
Are you angry that I forsake you all and our Lord?

When food falls from my mouth, I don't leave
a plate, glass and candle to light your way,
and I know, oh Lord, I know these old ways.
Aunty, I will light candles and call all your names:
Aunty Rita, Mammy Joyce, Uncle Peter, Granny.

Brixton Market

I would stand at market stalls
and watch her take days to pick,
how she would test the okra,
bending their tips, placing only
the ones that snapped into a brown paper bag;
the way she scrutinised the yam,
feeling and weighing it in her palm;
plantains picked one by one
like an artist selecting her tools.
Flawed produce would be haggled
to the last, and sometimes
she would turn her back and walk
to make her point and get her way.
I pulled that shopping trolley
into the stench of meat shops,
waiting as she pointed to red slabs
she wanted. How many times
would she point and weigh
to change her mind!
I would stare at the goose-bumped
boiling chicken hanging from ceiling,
the cow-foot, and severed pig tails.
I tried to hold my breath at the fish stall
as she chose the kippers, and we waited
for the snapper to be cleaned.
At Kwik Save, each can of baked beans
was vetted for dents, each egg
delicately lifted, searched for cracks.
I would learn that this is how my grandmother

taught her, kneeling in the bush uprooting dasheen
on the family land. She, too, hawk-eyed,
tested each provision to know
what was ripe, ready and good to cook.

The House on Jubilee Street

The roof leaks golden brown dust,
like the sugar deadly for your diabetes.
Clean laundry is still piled on your bed.
The wardrobe shows your ageing seasons:
from flares and minis, to long pleated skirts
and silk petticoats folded neatly on the shelves.
Your bottom is indented in the cushion
of your favourite chair. A faded palm cross
hangs on the living-room wall;
tiles detach from the verandah floor;
downstairs the wood column rots.
Seven Septembers since you died,
yet no one will give the house
its last rite, and so it remains,
woodworm gnawing the roof;
everything fixed for your resurrection.

Our Last Supper

1

There are flickering tea lights on each table.
I am on stage. Suddenly there you are
in the front row, clutching your grandchild,
both of you the same age as when you died.
You are the fragile sparrow, the dull wren,
head tied in silk scarf like an old Russian peasant.
You are flounce and long-length pleated skirts
and I can see your ankles – those bird legs
still don't look able to take your weight.
You are holding the little boy in your lap.
He is Grandma's darling and you are not dead.
He clutches your hands. Here is pure love.
Each word from my rustling page meets
your little nod. You are virgin audience,
who never saw me read. I am sure this
is a dream, you sitting here so serene,
your smile saying I see you now, I see
you; and I become your preening peacock.

2

We leave the poetry event to eat.
It's that same last meal, again and again.
It's plantain slices with fresh coconut bakes.
You eat tomatoes peeled and thinly diced, I eat
spicy baked beans. You sip rich cocoa tea,
I pick out the fish bones for the baby.
I am proud of you: your voice is spring water,
bubbly and alive. We hold hands,
the baby's palms squeezed flat between ours
like a group prayer. This is red lily love.
Then a knife clatters from another table
in the empty restaurant. I wake up
and you are gone. I always want to raise
you from the dead. It is another morning,
you have gone again. I am nothing. Even
in this dream I never get to say goodbye.

How Our Bodies Did This Unfamiliar Thing

We women stand in our men shoes, our bodies
doing this unfamiliar thing. Hands that scrubbed
clothes in wash basins, wrung pillowcases, hung white
flannel sheets on long clothes lines, pinning and clipping,
how now those hands have become cranes, each hand
a link in a chain, joining steel feathers, building birds
of prey. It was the world turned inside out. It was
a time when birds migrated here from Germany
to hunt prey. Each lift of arm a piece of the jigsaw,
build muscles on our puny arms. The lift – slot, lift
– slot, lift – slot, seven days for three years. My fingers
would crush my pay slips, fold fresh notes, slip each
between my breast, burying my independence in the folds
of my body. How our bones rose up in dark times and held
the hounds at bay. How our bodies fed the children, how we
endured. How we grew wings in these dark times
and when our men returned they hacked off our wings
with hatchets and folded us back into the kitchen.

Lot's Wife Speaks

That day my heart turned bitter karali.
That night they howled like rabid dogs
and pungent sulphur burned my nostrils.
I looked at my bleach floor and wept,
stood kneading the bread dough, till my hands
bled, pounding flesh over and over.
How Lot could sit and lick down domino
with them angels! I keep telling Lot,
every day bucket go ah well, one day
bam bam go stick. I say Lot boy fling out
some strong rum nuh, that go do the trick.
Drunk them into stupid sleep. I shout out
the window to that mob of carrion crow
come to gorge on innocence, *Allyuh come nuh,*
come you go see! I pulled my girls close, our shield
of three as joyful as trapped prey. We hugged up
and sank through the kitchen floor to rest we body
on moist earth. I say to myself, if he try and push
my girls out there tonight, is me and he in here,
angels or no damn angels. Then I got on my knees
and offered myself seasoned with salt, so they could be
refused. So they could have choice. Man,
pleading words vomit out of my mouth that night
as my knees bled so my daughters could blossom.
Then I who bent to no one, bowed my head
to the Lord and uttered, *Toda Lecha, Toda Lecha,*
Oh Lord Toda Lecha, till the night said, *Hush*
now woman, hush up, he hear you, we all hear you.
And as night spoke my heart turn hibiscus there and then.

My Humble Beseech

Oh Sacred Heart, I did not want her to die
so I asked what I could do. Gather, she said,
gather, the nails that fixed him on that cross,
the imprint of Mary's feet in the dirt, the tears
of the disciples, the rumble of the big stone
as it rolled to block the tomb. Gather, she said,
the sea salt pitched on the shore of Galilee, when
the sea wept, gather them all for your intercession.
I cannot, I said, that was too long ago. Well gather
tears of the wretched prisoners on death row,
gather their last confessions, gather the tears
of Virgin Mary dolls in Haiti, gather the prayers
of mothers for their dead babies. I cannot, I said.
Well look for death's twin, a burnished butterfly
man with a top hat, naked, wearing a red loin cloth.
Where can I find him? Search in your dreams,
she said. So I searched for forty days and nights.
I searched in vain. I called to him with tears
and white candles by my bed. I cannot find him, I said,
he will not show himself to me. Then death will come
like a lover, she said, he will take her gently.
What can I do? Let go, she said. Let go.

Sharon Olds

The Sisters of Sexual Treasure

As soon as my sister and I got out of our
mother's house, all we wanted to
do was fuck, obliterate
her tiny sparrow body and narrow
grasshopper legs. The men's bodies
were like our father's body! The massive
hocks, flanks, thighs, male
structure of the hips, knees, calves –
we could have him there, the steep forbidden
buttocks, backs of the knees, the cock
in our mouth, ah the cock in our mouth.
                    Like explorers who
discover a lost city, we went
nuts with joy, undressed the men
slowly and carefully, as if
uncovering buried artifacts that
proved our theory of the lost culture:
that if Mother said it wasn't there,
it was there.

The Language of the Brag

I have wanted excellence in the knife-throw,
I have wanted to use my exceptionally strong and accurate arms
and my straight posture and quick electric muscles
to achieve something at the center of a crowd,
the blade piercing the bark deep,
the haft slowly and heavily vibrating like the cock.

I have wanted some epic use for my excellent body,
some heroism, some American achievement
beyond the ordinary for my extraordinary self,
magnetic and tensile, I have stood by the sandlot
and watched the boys play.

I have wanted courage, I have thought about fire
and the crossing of waterfalls, I have dragged around

my belly big with cowardice and safety,
stool charcoal from the iron pills,
huge breasts leaking colostrum,
legs swelling, hands swelling,
face swelling and reddening, hair
falling out, inner sex
stabbed again and again with pain like a knife.
I have lain down.

I have lain down and sweated and shaken
and passed blood and shit and water and
slowly alone in the center of a circle I have
passed the new person out
and they have lifted the new person free of the act
and wiped the new person free of that
language of blood like praise all over the body.

I have done what you wanted to do, Walt Whitman,
Allen Ginsberg, I have done this thing,
I and the other women this exceptional
act with the exceptional heroic body,
this giving birth, this glistening verb,
and I am putting my proud American boast
right here with the others.

The Pope's Penis

It hangs deep in his robes, a delicate
clapper at the center of a bell.
It moves when he moves, a ghostly fish in a
halo of silver seaweed, the hair
swaying in the dimness and the heat – and at night,
while his eyes sleep, it stands up
in praise of God.

New Mother

A week after our child was born,
you cornered me in the spare room
and we sank down on the bed.
You kissed me and kissed me, my milk undid its
burning slipknot through my nipples,
soaking my shirt. All week I had smelled of milk,
fresh milk, sour. I began to throb:
my sex had been torn easily as cloth by the
crown of her head, I'd been cut with a knife and
sewn, the stitches pulling at my skin – and the
first time you're broken, you don't know
you'll be healed again, better than before.
I lay in fear and blood and milk
while you kissed and kissed me, your lips hot and swollen
as a teenage boy's, your sex dry and big,
all of you so tender, you hung over me,
over the nest of the stitches, over the
splitting and tearing, with the patience of someone who
finds a wounded animal in the woods
and stays with it, not leaving its side
until it is whole, until it can run again.

On the Subway

The young man and I face each other.
His feet are huge, in black sneakers
laced with white in a complex pattern like a
set of intentional scars. We are stuck on
opposite sides of the car, a couple of
molecules stuck in a rod of energy
rapidly moving through darkness. He has
or my white eye imagines he has
the casual cold look of a mugger,
alert under lowered eyelids. He is wearing
red, like the inside of the body
exposed. I am wearing old fur, the
whole skin of an animal taken
and used. I look at his unknown face,
he looks at my grandmother's coat, and I don't
know if I am in his power —
he could take my coat so easily, my
briefcase, my life —
or if he is in my power, the way I am
living off his life, eating the steak
he may not be eating, as if I am taking
the food from his mouth. And he is black
and I am white, and without meaning or
trying to I must profit from our history,
the way he absorbs the murderous beams of the
nation's heart, as black cotton
absorbs the heat of the sun and holds it. There is
no way to know how easy this
white skin makes my life, this
life he could break so easily, the way I
think his own back is being broken, the
rod of his soul that at birth was dark and
fluid, rich as the heart of a seedling
ready to thrust up into any available light.

The Feelings

When the intern listened to the stopped heart
I stared at him, as if he or I
were wild, were from some other world, I had
lost the language of gestures, I could not
know what it meant for a stranger to push
the gown up along the body of my father.
My face was wet, my father's face
was faintly moist with the sweat of his life,
the last moments of hard work.
I was leaning against the wall, in the corner, and
he lay on the bed, we were both doing something,
and everyone else in the room believed in the Christian God,
they called my father *the shell on the bed*, I was the
only one there who knew
he was entirely gone, the only one
there to say goodbye to his body
that was all he was, I held, hard,
to his foot, I thought of the Inuit elder
holding the stern of the death canoe, I
let him out slowly into the physical world.
I felt the dryness of his lips under
my lips, I felt how even my slight
kiss moved his head on the pillow
the way things move as if on their own in shallow water,
I felt his hair rush through my fingers
like a wolf's, the walls shifted, the floor, the
ceiling wheeled as if I was not
walking out of the room but the room was
backing away around me. I would have
liked to stay beside him, ride by his
shoulder while they drove him to the place where they would
    burn him,

see him safely into the fire,
touch his ashes in their warmth, and bring my
finger to my tongue. The next morning,
I felt my husband's body on me
crushing me sweetly like a weight laid heavy on some
soft thing, some fruit, holding me
hard to this world. Yes the tears came
out like juice and sugar from the fruit –
the skin thins, and breaks, and rips, there are
laws on this earth, and we live by them.

My Father Speaks to Me from the Dead

I seem to have woken up in a pot-shed,
on clay, on shards, the glitter paths
of slugs kiss-crossing my body. I don't know
where to start, with this grime on me.
I take the spider glue-net, plug
of the dead, out of my mouth, let's see
if where I have been I can do this.
I love your feet. I love your knees,
I love your our my legs, they are so
long because they are yours and mine
both. I love your – what can I call it,
between your legs, we never named it, the
glint and purity of its curls. I love
your rear end, I changed you once,
washed the detritus off your tiny
bottom, with my finger rubbed
the oil on you; when I touched your little
anus I crossed wires with God for a moment.
I never hated your shit – that was
your mother. I love your navel, thistle
seed fossil, even though
it's her print on you. Of course I love
your breasts – did you see me looking up
from within your daughter's face, as she nursed?
I love your bony shoulders and you know I
love your hair, thick and live
as earth. And I never hated your face,
I hated its eruptions. You know what I love?
I love your brain, its halves and silvery
folds, like a woman's labia.
I love in you
even what comes

from deep in your mother – your heart, that hard worker,
and your womb, it is a heaven to me,
I lie on its gentle hills and gaze up
at its rosy vault.
I have been in a body without breath,
I have been in the morgue, in fire, in the slagged
chimney, in the air over the earth,
and buried in the earth, and pulled down
into the ocean – where I have been
I understand this life, I am matter,
your father, I made you, when I say now that I love you
I mean look down at your hand, move it,
that action is matter's love, for human
love go elsewhere.

I Go Back to May 1937

I see them standing at the formal gates of their colleges,
I see my father strolling out
under the ochre sandstone arch, the
red tiles glinting like bent
plates of blood behind his head, I
see my mother with a few light books at her hip
standing at the pillar made of tiny bricks,
the wrought-iron gate still open behind her, its
sword-tips aglow in the May air,
they are about to graduate, they are about to get married,
they are kids, they are dumb, all they know is they are
innocent, they would never hurt anybody.
I want to go up to them and say Stop,
don't do it – she's the wrong woman,
he's the wrong man, you are going to do things
you cannot imagine you would ever do,
you are going to do bad things to children,
you are going to suffer in ways you have not heard of,
you are going to want to die. I want to go
up to them there in the late May sunlight and say it,
her hungry pretty face turning to me,
her pitiful beautiful untouched body,
his arrogant handsome face turning to me,
his pitiful beautiful untouched body,
but I don't do it. I want to live. I
take them up like the male and female
paper dolls and bang them together
at the hips, like chips of flint, as if to
strike sparks from them, I say
Do what you are going to do, and I will tell about it.

Calvinist Parents

'Sometime during the Truman Administration, Sharon Olds's parents tied her to a chair, and she is still writing about it.'
— *review of* The Unswept Room

'My father was a gentleman, and he expected us to be gentlemen. If we did not observe the niceties of etiquette he whopped us with his belt. He had a strong arm, and boy did we feel it.'
— *Prescott Sheldon Bush, brother to a president and uncle to another*

They put roofs over our heads.
Ours was made of bent tiles,
so the edge of the roof had a broken look,
as if a lot of crockery
had been thrown down, onto the home –
a dump for heaven's cheap earthenware.
Along the eaves, the arches were like
entries to the Colosseum
where a lion might appear, or an eight-foot armored
being with the painted face
of a simpering lady. Bees would not roost
in those concave combs, above our rooms,
birds not swarm. How does a young 'un
pay for room and board – by belt,
by hairbrush, by 2 × 4. They put a
roof over our heads, against lightning,
and droppings – no foreign genes, no outside
gestures, no unfamilial words;
and under that roof, they labored as they had been
labored over, they beat us into swords.

The Bra

It happened, with me, on the left side, first,
I would look down, and the soft skin of the
nipple had become like a blister, as if it had been
lifted by slow puffs of breath
from underneath. It took weeks, months,
a year. And those white harnesses,
like contagion masks for conjoined twins
– if you saw a strap showing, on someone
you knew well enough, you could whisper, in her ear,
It's Snowing Up North. There were bowers to walk through
home from school, trellis arches
like aboveground tunnels, froths of leaves –
that spring, no one was in them, except,
sometimes, a glimpse of police. They found
her body in the summer, the girl in our class
missing since winter, in the paper they printed
the word in French, *brassiere*, I felt a little
glad she had still been wearing it,
as if a covering, of any
kind, could be a hopeless dignity.
But now they are saying that her bra was buried
in the basement of his house – when she was pulled down into
the ground, she was naked. For a moment I am almost half
glad they tore him apart with Actaeon
electric savaging. In the photo,
the shoulder straps seem to be making
wavering O's, and the sorrow's cups
are O's, and the bands around to the hook
and eye in the back make a broken O.
It looks like something taken down
to the bones – God's apron – God eviscerated –
its plain, cotton ribbons rubbed

with earth. When he said, In as much as ye have
done it unto one of the least
of these my brethren, ye have done it unto
me, he meant girls – or if he'd known better
he would have meant girls.

His Costume

Somehow I never stopped to notice
that my father liked to dress as a woman.
He had his sign language about women
talking too much, and being stupid,
but whenever there was a costume party
he would dress like us, the tennis balls
for breasts – balls for breasts – the pageboy
blond wig, the lipstick, he would sway
his body with moves of gracefulness
as if one being could be the whole
universe, its ends curving back to come
up from behind it. Six feet, and maybe
one-eighty, one-ninety, he had the shapely
legs of a male Grable – in a short
skirt, he leaned against a bookcase pillar
nursing his fifth drink, gazing
around from inside his mascara purdah
with those salty eyes. The woman from next door
had a tail and ears, she was covered with Reynolds Wrap,
she was Kitty Foil, and my mother was in
a teeny tuxedo, but he always won
the prize. Those nights, he had a look of daring,
as if he was getting away with something,
a look of triumph, of having stolen
back. And as far as I knew, he never threw
up as a woman, or passed out, or made
those signals of scorn with his hands, just leaned,
voluptuous, at ease, deeply
present, as if sensing his full potential, crossing
over into himself, and back,
over and back.

19

When we took the acid, his wife was off
with someone else, there was a hole in their bedroom
wall where the Steuben wedding owl
had flown from one room right through into another,
I was in love with his best friend, who had
gone into a monastery
after he'd deflowered me, so we
knew each other: when he finished, under
my palm, I could feel the circular ribs of his
penis; I finished with my legs wrapped around his
leg, even with my toes pointed, my
feet reached only halfway down
his calf, later I was lying on the bathroom
floor, looking up at him, naked, he was
6'6", a decathlete,
my eyes followed the inner line of his
leg, up, up, up,
up, up, up, up.
Weeks later, he would pull a wall-phone
out of a wall, he would cross the divider
in his Mustang at 2 a.m. with me and go
sixty, against traffic, crying, I could
hardly hear what he said about the barbed
wire and his father and his balls – but that
acid night, we stayed up all night, I was
not in love with him, so his beauty made me
happy, we chattered, we chatted naked, he
told me everything he liked
about my body – and he liked everything –
even the tiny gooseflesh bumps
around my hard nipples,
he said the way to make love to me

would be from behind, with that sheer angle, his
forefinger drew it, gently, the extreme
hairpin curve of the skinny buttocks,
he said it the way I thought an older
cousin in a dream might give advice
to a younger cousin, his fingertip
barely missing my — whatever, in love, one would
call the asshole — he regarded me with a
savoring kindness, from a cleft of sweet lust in the
human he actually looked at me
and thought how I best should be fucked. *Oooh.*
Oooh. It meant there was something to be done with me,
something exactly right, he looked at me
and saw it,
willing to not be the one
who did it — all night, he desired me and
protected me, he gazed at my body and un-
saw my parents' loathing, pore by
pore on my skin he closed that couple's eyes.

The Riser

When I heard that my mother had stood up after her near
death of toxic shock, at first
I could not get that supine figure in my
mind's eye to rise, she had been so
flat, her face shiny as the ironing board's
gray asbestos cover. Once my
father had gone that horizontal, he did
not lift up, again, until he was
fire. But my mother put her fine legs
over the side, got her soles
on the floor, slowly poured her body from the
mattress into the vertical, she
stood between nurse and husband, and they let
go, for a second – alive, upright,
my primate! When I'd last seen her, she was silver
and semi-liquid, like something ladled
onto the sheet, early form
of shimmering life, amoeba or dazzle of
jism, and she'd tried to speak, like matter
trying to speak. Now she stands by the bed,
gaunt, slightly luminous, the
hospital gown hanging in blue
folds, like the picture of Jesus-come-back
in my choir book. She seemed to feel close to Jesus,
she loved the way he did not give up,
nothing could stop his love, he stood there
teetering beside the stone bed and he
folded his grave-clothes.

Bathing the New Born

I love with an almost fearful love
to remember the first baths I gave him,
our second child, so I knew what to do,
I laid the little torso along
my left forearm, nape of the neck
in the crook of my elbow, hips nearly as
small as a least tern's tail
against my wrist, thigh held loosely
in the loop of thumb and forefinger, the
sign that means exactly right. I'd soap him,
the violet, cold feet, the scrotum
wrinkled as a waved whelk, the chest,
hands, clavicles, throat, gummy
furze of the scalp. When I got him too soapy he'd
slide in my grip like an armful of buttered
noodles, but I'd hold him not too tight,
I felt that I was good for him,
I'd tell him about his wonderful body
and the wonderful soap, and he'd look up at me,
one week old, his eyes still wide
and apprehensive. I love that time
when you croon and croon to them, you can see
the calm slowly entering them, you can
sense it in your clasping hand,
the loose spine relaxing against
the muscle of your forearm, you feel the fear
leaving their bodies, he lay in the blue
oval plastic baby tub and
looked at me in wonder and began to
move his silky limbs at will in the water.

The Clasp

She was four, he was one, it was raining, we had colds,
we had been in the apartment two weeks straight,
I grabbed her to keep her from shoving him over on his
face, again, and when I had her wrist
in my grasp I compressed it, fiercely, for almost a
second, to make an impression on her,
to hurt her, our beloved firstborn, I even nearly
savored the stinging sensation of the squeezing, the
expression, into her, of my anger,
'Never, never again', the righteous
chant accompanying the clasp. It happened very
fast – grab, crush, crush,
crush, release – and at the first extra
force, she swung her head, as if checking
who this was, and looked at me,
and saw me – yes, this was her mom,
her mom was doing this. Her dark,
deeply open eyes took me
in, she knew me, in the shock of the moment
she learned me. This was her mother, one of the
two whom she most loved, the two
who loved her most, near the source of love
was this.

Bible Study: 71 B.C.E.

After Marcus Licinius Crassus
defeated the army of Spartacus,
he crucified 6,000 men.
That is what the records say,
as if he drove in the 18,000
nails himself. I wonder how
he felt, that day, if he went outside
among them, if he walked that human
woods. I think he stayed in his tent
and drank, and maybe copulated,
hearing the singing being done for him,
the woodwind-tuning he was doing at one
remove, to the six-thousandth power.
And maybe he looked out, sometimes,
to see the rows of instruments,
his orchard, the earth bristling with it
as if a patch in his brain had itched
and this was his way of scratching it
directly. Maybe it gave him pleasure,
and a sense of balance, as if he had suffered,
and now had found redress for it,
and voice for it. I speak as a monster,
someone who today has thought at length
about Crassus, his ecstasy of feeling
nothing while so much is being
felt, his hot lightness of spirit
in being free to walk around
while others are nailed above the earth.
It may have been the happiest day
of his life. If he had suddenly cut
his hand on a wineglass, I doubt he would
have woken up to what he was doing.

It is frightening to think of him suddenly
seeing what he was, to think of him running
outside, to try to take them down,
one man to save 6,000.
If he could have lowered one,
and seen the eyes when the level of pain
dropped like a sudden soaring into pleasure,
wouldn't that have opened in him
the wild terror of understanding
the other? But then he would have had
5,999
to go. Probably it almost never
happens, that a Marcus Crassus
wakes. I think he dozed, and was roused
to his living dream, lifted the flap
and stood and looked out, at the rustling, creaking
living field – his, like an external
organ, a heart.

Physics

Her first puzzle had three pieces,
she'd take the last piece, and turn it,
and lower it in, like a sewer-lid,
flush with the street. The bases of the frames were like
wooden fur, guard-hairs sticking out
of the pelt. I'd set one on the floor and spread
the pieces out around it. It makes me
groan to think of Red Riding Hood's hood,
a single, scarlet, pointed piece, how
long since I have seen her. Later, panthers,
500 pieces, and an Annunciation,
1,000 pieces, we would gaze, on our elbows,
into its gaps. Now she tells me
that if I were sitting in a twenty-foot barn,
with the doors open at either end,
and a fifty-foot ladder hurtled through the barn
at the speed of light, there would be a moment
– after the last rung was inside the barn
and before the first rung came out the other end –
when the whole fifty-foot ladder would be
inside the twenty-foot barn, and I believe her,
I have thought her life was inside my life
like that. When she reads the college catalogues, I
look away and hum. I have not grown
up yet, I've lived as my daughter's mother
the way I had lived as my mother's daughter,
inside her life. I have not been born yet.

Psalm

Bending over, at the August table
where the summer towels are kept, putting
a stack on the bottom shelf, I felt his
kiss, in its shock of whiskers, on an inner
curve of that place I know by his knowing,
have seen with the vision of his touch. To be entered
thus, on a hip-high table piled with
sheaves of towels, bath and hand,
terry-cloth eden, is to feel at one's center
a core of liquid heat as if
one is an earth. Some time later,
we were kissing in near sleep, *I think
we did it this time*, I whispered, *I think
we're joined at the hip.* He has a smile sometimes
from the heart; at this hour, I live in its light.
I gnaw very gently on his jaw, *Would you want me to
eat you, in the Andes, in a plane crash,* I murmur,
to survive? Yes. We smile. He asks,
Would you want me to eat you to survive? I would love it,
I cry out. We almost sleep, there is a series of
arms around us and between us, in sets,
touches given as if received. *Did you think
we were going to turn into each other?*, and I get
one of those smiles, as if his face
is a speckled, rubbled, sandy, satiny
cactus-flower eight inches across.
Yes, he whispers. I know he is humoring,
rote sweet-talking. A sliver of late
sun is coming through, between the curtains,
it illumines the scaly surfaces
of my knuckles, its line like a needle held,
to cleanse it, above a match. I move

my wedding finger to stand in the slit
of flame. From the ring's curve there rises
a fan of borealis fur
like the first instant of sunrise. Do not
tell me this could end. Do not tell me.

from War

5. WHEN HE CAME FOR THE FAMILY

They looked at their daughter standing with her music
in her hand, the page covered with dots and
lines, with its shared language. They knew
families had been taken. What they did not know
was the way he would pick her cello up
by the scroll neck and take its amber
torso-shape and lift it and break it
against the fireplace. The brickwork crushed the
close-grained satiny wood, they stood and
stared at him.

11. HIS CREW

Burning, he kept the plane up
long enough for the crew to jump. He could
feel the thrust down, and the lift,
each time one of them leapt, full-term, the
parachutes unfolding and glistening, little
sacs of afterbirth. They drifted toward
what could be long lives, his fist
seared to the stick. When he'd felt all six
leave him, he put the nose down
and saw the earth coming up toward him,
green as a great basin of water
being lifted to his face.

Material Ode

O tulle, O taffeta, O grosgrain –
I call upon you now, girls,
of fabrics and the woman I sing. My husband
had said he was probably going to leave me – not
for sure, but likely, maybe – and no, it did not
have to do with her. O satin, O
sateen, O velvet, O fucking velveeta –
the day of the doctors' dress-up dance,
the annual folderol, the lace,
the net, he said it would be hard for her
to see me there, dancing with him,
would I mind not going. And since I'd been
for thirty years enarming him,
I enarmed him further – *Arma Virumque*,
sackcloth, ashen embroidery! As he
put on his tux, I saw his slight
smirk into the mirror, as he did his bow tie,
but after more than three decades, you have some
affection for each other's little faults,
and it suited me to cherish the belief
no meanness could happen between us. Fifty-
fifty we had made the marriage,
fifty-fifty its demise. And when he came
home and shed his skin, Reader,
I slept with him, thinking it meant
he was back, his body was speaking for him,
and as it spoke, its familiar sang
from the floor, the old-boy tie. O silk,
O slub, O cocoon stolen. It is something
our species does, isn't it,
we take what we can. Or else there'd be grubs
who kept people, in rooms, to produce

placentas for the larvae's use, there would be
a cow who would draw from our wombs our unborn
offspring, to make of them shoes for a calf.
O bunny-pyjamas of children! Love
where loved. O babies' flannel sleeper
with a slice of cherry pie on it.
Love only where loved! O newborn suit
with a smiling worm over the heart, it is
forbidden to love where we are not loved.

The Worst Thing

One side of the highway, the waterless hills.
The other, in the distance, the tidal wastes,
estuaries, bay, throat
of the ocean. I had not put it into
words, yet – the worst thing,
but I thought that I could say it, if I said it
word by word. My friend was driving,
sea-level, coastal hills, valley,
foothills, mountains – the slope, for both,
of our earliest years. I had been saying
that it hardly mattered to me now, the pain,
what I minded was – say there was
a god – of love – and I'd given – I had meant
to give – my life – to it – and I
had failed, well I could just suffer for that
but what, if I,
had harmed, love? I howled this out,
and on my glasses the salt water pooled, almost
sweet to me, then, because it was named,
the worst thing – and once it was named,
I knew there was no god, there were only
people. And my friend reached over,
to where my fists clutched each other,
and the back of his hand rubbed them, a second,
with clumsiness, with the courtesy
of no eros, the homemade kindness.

Maritime

Some mornings, the hem of the forewash had been almost
golden, alaskas and berings of foam
pulled along the tensile casing.
Often the surface was a ship's grey,
a destroyer's, flecks of sun, jellies,
sea stars, blood stars, men and women of war,
weed Venus hair. A month a year,
for thirty years. Nine hundred mornings,
sometimes we could tell, from the beach,
while taking our clothes off, how cold the water
was, by looking at it – and then,
at its icy touch, the nipples took
their barnacle glitter, underwater
a soft frigor bathed the sex as if
drawing her detailed outline in the seeing
brain, and he braced his knees in the press
of the swell, and I dove under, and near the
floor of this life I glided between his ankles, not
knowing, until he was behind me, if I had got
through without brushing them. Then,
the getting out, rising, half-poached
egg coming up out of its shell and membrane,
weight of the breasts finding their float-point
on the air, soppy earths, all this
in the then beloved's gaze,
the ball in the socket at the top of his thighbone
like a marrow eye through which the foreshore could have
seen us, his hip joints like the gravital centres
of my spirit. Then we'd lie, feet toward the Atlantic,
my hypothermic claw tucked
beneath the heat of his flank, under
day moon, or coming storm,

swallow, heron, prism-bow, drizzle,
osprey, test-pilot out to No Man's.
And then, before our sight, the half world
folded on itself, and bent, and swallowed,
and opened, again, its wet, long
mouths, and drank itself.

One Secret Thing

One secret thing happened
at the end of my mother's life, when I was
alone with her. I knew it should happen —
I knew someone was there, in there,
something less unlike my mother than
anything else on earth. And the jar
was there on the table, the space around it
pulled back from it, like the awestruck handmade
air around the crèche, and her open
mouth was parched. It was late. The lid
eased off. I watched my finger draw through
the jelly, its egg-sex essence, the four
corners of the room were not creatures, were not
the four winds of the earth, if I did not
do this, what was I — I rubbed the cowlick of
petrolatum on the skin around where the
final measures of what was almost not
breath swayed, and her throat made a guttural
creek bed sound, like pebbly relief. But each
lip was stuck by chap to its row
of teeth, stuck fast. And then I worked
for my motherhood, my humanhood, I
slid my forefinger slowly back and
forth, along the scab-line and underlying
canines and incisors, upper lip and then
lower lip, until, like a basted
seam, softly ripped, what had been
joined was asunder, I ran the salve inside the folds, along the gums,
common mercy. The secret was
how deeply I did not want to touch
inside her, and how much the act
was an act of escape, my last chance
to free myself.

Self-Portrait, Rear View

At first, I do not believe it, in the hotel
triple mirror, that that is my body, in
back, below the waist, and above
the legs – the thing that doesn't stop moving
when I stop moving.
And it doesn't look like just one thing,
or even one big, double thing
– even the word saddlebags has a
smooth, calfskin feel to it,
compared to this compendium
of net string bags shaking their booty of
cellulite fruits and nuts. Some lumps
look like bonbons translated intact
from chocolate box to buttocks, the curl on top
showing, slightly, through my skin. Once I see what I can
do with this, I do it, high-stepping
to make the rapids of my bottom rush
in ripples like a world wonder. Slowly,
I believe what I am seeing, a 54-year-old
rear end, once a tight end,
high and mighty, almost a chicken butt, now
exhausted, as if tragic. But this is not
an invasion, my cul-de-sac is not being
used to hatch alien cells, ball peens,
gyroscopes, sacks of marbles. It's my hoard
of treasure, my good luck, not to be
dead, yet, though when I flutter
the wing of my ass again, and see,
in a clutch of eggs, each egg,
on its own, as if shell-less, shudder, I wonder
if anyone has ever died,
looking in a mirror, of horror. I think I will

not even catch a cold from it,
I will go to school to it, to Butt
Boot Camp, to the video store, where I saw,
in the window, my hero, my workout jelly
role model, my apotheosis: *Killer Buns.*

Red Sea

And at a party, or in any crowd, years
after he has left, there will come an almost
visible image of my ex, appearing
at the far side of a room, moving
toward me, making his way between people,
as the soul used to make its way, through
clothes, until it lay, bare,
beside the soul of the beloved, then they seemed
to swim into each other, and they sang. Before me,
on either side, facing each other
like opposing armies, two columns
of words keen and catcall to each other:

relinquishment,	fastening,
abjure,	trice up;
forfeiture,	colligate,
disclaim,	padlock;
free,	ligate,
abandon,	yoke,
desert,	surcingle,
secede,	belay;
quit,	solder,
yield,	snood,
leave,	enchain,
release,	bind;
	clinch,
	latchet,
	suture,
	peg;
	splice,
	wattle,
	harness,
	nail,

much work to be done. And Love said, to me,
What if I, myself, asked you
to love him less. And I stepped out into
the trough between the pillars, the dry
ground through the midst of the sea — the waters
a wall unto me, on the right hand,
and on the left.

Poem of Thanks

Years later, long single,
I want to turn to his departed back,
and say, What gifts we had of each other!
What pleasure – confiding, open-eyed,
fainting with what we were allowed to stay up
late doing. And you couldn't say,
could you, that the touch you had from me
was other than the touch of one
who could love for life – whether we were suited
or not – for *life*, like a sentence. And now that I
consider, the touch that I had from you
became not the touch of the long view, but like the
tolerant willingness of one
who is passing through. Colleague of sand
by moonlight – and by beach noonlight, once,
and of straw, salt bale in a barn, and mulch
inside a garden, between the rows – once
partner of up against the wall in that tiny
bathroom with the lock that fluttered like a chrome
butterfly beside us, hip-height, the familiar
of our innocence, which was the ignorance
of what would be asked, what was required,
thank you for every hour. And I
accept your thanks, as if it were
a gift of yours, to give them – let's part
equals, as we were in every bed, pure
equals of the earth.

Ode to the Hymen

I don't know when you came into being,
inside me, when I was inside my mother –
maybe when the involuntary
muscles were setting, like rose jello.
I love to think of you then, so whole, so
impervious, you and the clitoris as
safe as the life in which you were housed, they would have
had to kill both my mother and me
to get at either of you. I love her, at this
moment, as the big fortress around me, the
matronhead around the sweetmeat
of my maidenhead. I don't know who
invented you – to keep a girl's inwards
clean and well-cupboarded. Dear wall,
dear gate, dear stile, dear Dutch door, not a
cat-flap nor a swinging door
but a one-time piñata. How many places in the
body were made to be destroyed
once? You were very sturdy, weren't you,
you took your job seriously – I'd never
felt such pain – you were the woman
the magician saws in two. I was proud of you,
turning to a cupful of the bright arterial
ingredient. And how lucky we were,
you and I, that we got to choose
when, and with whom, and where, and why – plush
pincushion, somehow related
to statues that wept. It happened on the rug
of a borrowed living room, but I felt
as if we were in Diana's woods –
he, and I, and you, together,
or as if we were where the magma from the core of the

earth burst up through the floor of the sea.
Thank you for your life and death,
thank you for your flower-girl walk
before me, throwing down your scarlet
petals. It would be years before
I married – years before I carried, within me,
a tiny, baby hymen, near the
eggs with other teentsy hymens
within them – but you unscrolled the carpet,
leading me into the animal life
of a woman. You were a sort of blood
mother to me: first you held me
close, for 18 years, and then
you let me go.

Warsan Shire

Our Blue Bodies

I have dreamt of you suspended
in amniotic fluid, your hair fanned
out and alive, long again, before the cancer.
Undying, our movements synchronised,
us, tied together at the navel,
umbilical cord and all its length tugging
at me, far as it might extend. Gregory Porter climbing
through *there will be no love that's dying*
here – his voice, and how it soothes you from
beyond the distant wall of this maybe womb,
the faint rhythm of a bigger heart
above us.

The House

i

Mother says there are locked rooms inside all women.
Kitchen of lust, bedroom of grief, bathroom of apathy.
Sometimes, the men – they come with keys,
and sometimes, the men – they come with hammers.

ii

Nin soo joog laga waayo, soo jiifso aa laga helaa,
I said *Stop*, I said *No* and he did not listen.

iii

Perhaps she has a plan, perhaps she takes him back to hers
so he can wake hours later, with a dry mouth, in a bathtub
full of ice, looking down at his new, neat procedure.

iv

I point to my body and say *Oh this old thing? No, I just slipped
it on.*

v

Are you going to eat that? I say to my mother, pointing to my
father who is lying on the dining room table, his mouth stuffed
with a red apple.

vi

The bigger my body is, the more locked rooms there are, the
more men come with keys. Ahmed didn't push it all the way in,
I still think about what he could have opened up inside of me.
B. came and hesitated at the door for three years. Jonny with

the blue eyes came with a bag of tools he had used on other women: one hairpin, a bottle of bleach, a switchblade and a jar of Vaseline. Yusuf called out God's name through the keyhole and no one answered. Some begged, some climbed the side of my body looking for a window, some said they were on their way and did not come.

vii

Show us on the doll where you were touched, they said.
I said *I don't look like a doll, I look like a house.*
They said *Show us on the house.*

Like this: two fingers in the jam jar
Like this: an elbow in the bathwater
Like this: a hand in the drawer.

viii

I should tell you about my first love who found a trapdoor under my left breast nine years ago, fell in and hasn't been seen since. Every now and then I feel something crawling up my thigh. He should make himself known. I'd probably let him out. I hope he hasn't bumped into the others, the missing boys from small towns, with pleasant mothers, who did bad things and got lost in the maze of my hair. I treat them well enough, a slice of bread, if they're lucky a piece of fruit. Except for Jonny with the blue eyes, who picked my locks and crawled in. Silly boy chained to the basement of my fears, I play music to drown him out.

ix

Knock knock.
Who's there?
No one.

x

At parties I point to my body and say *This is where love comes to die. Welcome, come in, make yourself at home.* Everyone laughs, they think I'm joking.

Backwards

The poem can start with him walking backwards into a room.
He takes off his jacket and sits down for the rest of his life,
that's how we bring Dad back.
I can make the blood run back up my nose, ants rushing into
    a hole.
We grow into smaller bodies, my breasts disappear,
your cheeks soften, teeth sink back into gums.
I can make us loved, just say the word.
Give them stumps for hands if even once they touched us
    without consent,
I can write the poem and make it disappear.
Step-Dad spits liquor back into glass,
Mum's body rolls back up the stairs, the bone pops back into
    place,
maybe she keeps the baby.
Maybe we're okay kid?
I'll rewrite this whole life and this time there'll be so much
    love,
you won't be able to see beyond it.

You won't be able to see beyond it,
I'll rewrite this whole life and this time there'll be so much
    love.
Maybe we're okay kid,
maybe she keeps the baby.
Mum's body rolls back up the stairs, the bone pops back into
    place,
Step-Dad spits liquor back into glass.
I can write the poem and make it disappear,
give them stumps for hands if even once they touched us
    without consent,
I can make us loved, just say the word.

Your cheeks soften, teeth sink back into gums
we grow into smaller bodies, my breasts disappear.
I can make the blood run back up my nose, ants rushing into a
    hole,
that's how we bring Dad back.
He takes off his jacket and sits down for the rest of his life.
The poem can start with him walking backwards into a room.

Her Blue Body Full of Light

Can you believe I have cancer? Yosra asks,
a mug of tea between her hands,
almost laughing, hair cut close to her scalp.
I imagine the cancer auditioning
inside her body, tiny translucent slivers
of light weaving in and out of her abdomen
and uterus, travelling up and through her throat,
needlepoints of light, fireworks glimmering down, the body
burning into itself, deep sea blue inside
her body, her ribcage an aquarium,
the cancer spreading and spreading, deep space,
her throat a lava lamp, sparklers beneath breastbone –
a lightshow, a million tiny jellyfish, orchestral womb,
kaleidoscopic ovaries, disco ball heart,
her skin glowing and glowing,
lit from the inside.

Midnight in the Foreign Food Aisle

Dear Uncle, is everything you love foreign
or are you foreign to everything you love?
We're all animals and the body wants what it wants,
I know. The blonde said *Come in, take off
your coat* and *What do you want to drink?*
Love is not haram but after years of fucking
women who cannot pronounce your name,
you find yourself in the foreign food aisle,
beside the turmeric and the saffron,
pressing your face into the ground, praying
in a language you haven't used in years.

Souvenir

I think I brought the war with me
on my skin, a shroud
circling my skull, matter under my nails.
It sits at my feet while I watch TV.
I hear its damp breath in the background
of every phone call. I feel it sleeping
between us in the bed. It lathers
my back in the shower. It presses
itself against me at the bathroom sink.
At night, it passes me the pills, it holds
my hand, I never meet its gaze.

Nail Technician as Palm Reader

The nail technician pushes my cuticles
back, turns my hand over,
stretches the skin on my palm
and says *I see your daughters
and their daughters*.

That night, in a dream, the first girl emerges
from a slit in my stomach. The scar heals
into a smile. The man I love pulls the stitches out
with his fingernails. We leave black sutures
curling on the side of the bath.

I wake as the second girl crawls
head first up my throat –
a flower, blossoming
out of the hole in my face.

Grief Has Its Blue Hands in Her Hair

She sleeps all day,
dreams of you in both worlds,
tills the blood in and out of uterus,
wakes up smelling of zinc.

Grief sedated by orgasm,
orgasm heightened by grief.

God was in the room
when the man said to the woman
I love you so
much wrap your legs around
me pull me in pull me in pull
me in pullme in pull mein
pullmein.

Sometimes when he had her
nipple in his mouth she'd whisper
Allah –
this too is a form of worship.

It smelt like flowers the last time she
buried the friend with the kind eyes.
The last time she buried her face
into his mattress, *frangipani.*

Her hips grind,
pestle and mortar,
cinnamon and cloves.
Whenever he pulls out:
loss.

The Ugly Daughter

Knows loss intimately,
carries whole cities in her belly.

As a child, relatives wouldn't hold her.
She was splintered wood and sea water,
she reminded them of the war.

On her fifteenth birthday you taught her
how to tie her hair like rope
and smoke it over burning frankincense.

You made her gargle rosewater
and while she coughed, said
*Macaanto, girls shouldn't smell
of lonely or empty.*

You're her mother.
Why did you not warn her?
That she will not be loved
if she is covered in continents,
if her teeth are small colonies,
if her stomach is an island,
if her thighs are borders?

Who wants to lie down
and watch the world burn
in their bedroom?

Your daughter's face is a small riot,
her hands are a civil war,
a refugee camp behind each ear,
a body littered with ugly things

but God,
doesn't she wear
the world well.

Conversations About Home
(at the Deportation Centre)

*

Well, I think home spat me out, the blackouts and curfews like
tongue against loose tooth. God, do you know how difficult it
is, to talk about the day your own city dragged you by the hair,
past the old prison, past the school gates, past the burning
torsos erected on poles like flags? When I meet others like me
I recognise the longing, the missing, the memory of ash on
their faces. No one leaves home unless home is the mouth of a
shark. I've been carrying the old anthem in my mouth for so
long that there's no space for another song, another tongue or
another language. I know a shame that shrouds, totally engulfs.
Allah Ceebta, I tore up and ate my own passport in an airport
hotel. I'm bloated with language I can't afford to forget.

They ask me *how did you get here?* Can't you see it on my body? The desert red with immigrant bodies shot in the face for trying to enter, the Gulf of Aden bloated with immigrant bodies. I wouldn't put my children on the boat unless I thought the sea was safer than the land. I hope the journey meant more than miles because all of my children are in the water. I want to make love but my hair smells of war and running and running. Look at all these borders, foaming at the mouth with brown bodies broken and desperate. I'm the colour of hot sun on my face, my mother's remains were never buried. I spent days and nights in the stomach of the truck, I did not come out the same. Sometimes it feels like someone else is wearing my body.

I know a few things to be true. I do not know where I am going, where I have come from is disappearing, I am unwelcome and my beauty is not beauty here. My body is burning with the shame of not belonging, my body is longing. I am the sin of memory and the absence of memory. I watch the news and my mouth becomes a sink full of blood. The lines, the forms, the people at the desks, the calling cards, the immigration officers, the looks on the street, the cold settling deep into my bones, the English classes at night, the distance I am from home. But Alhamdulilah all of this is better than the scent of a woman completely on fire, or a truckload of men who look like my father, pulling out my teeth and nails, or fourteen men between my legs, or a gun, or a promise, or a lie, or his name, or his manhood in my mouth.

*

I hear them say, *go home*, I hear them say, *fucking immigrants, fucking refugees*. Are they really this arrogant? Do they not know that stability is like a lover with a sweet mouth upon your body one second and the next you are a tremor lying on the floor covered in rubble and old currency waiting for its return. All I can say is, I was once like you, the apathy, the pity, the ungrateful placement, and now my home is the mouth of a shark, now my home is the barrel of a gun. I'll see you on the other side.

Maymuun's Mouth

Maymuun lost her accent with the help of her local Community College. Most evenings she calls me long distance to discuss the pros and cons of heating molasses in the microwave to remove body hair. Her new voice is sophisticated. She has taken to dancing in front of strangers. She lives next door to a Dominican man who speaks to her in Spanish whenever they pass each other in hallways. I know she smiles at him, front teeth stained from the fluoride in the water back home. She's experiencing new things. We understand. We've received the photos of her standing by a bridge, the baby hairs she'd hated all her life slicked down on her forehead in intricate patterns. Last week her answering machine picked up. I imagined her hoisted by the waist, wearing stockings, learning to kiss with her new tongue.

Birds

Sofia used pigeon blood on her wedding night.
The next day, over the phone, she told me
how her husband smiled when he saw the sheets,

that he gathered them under his nose,
closed his eyes and dragged his tongue over the stain.
She mimicked his baritone, how he whispered

her name – *Safiya*,
pure, chaste, untouched.
We giggled over the static.

After he had praised her, she smiled, rubbed his head,
imagined his mother back home parading
these siren sheets through the town,

waving at balconies, torso swollen with pride,
her arms fleshy wings bound to her body,
ignorant of flight.

Fire

i

The morning you were made to leave
she sat on the front steps,
dress tucked between her thighs,
a packet of Marlboro Lights
near her bare feet, painting her nails
until the polish curdled.
Her mother phoned –

*What do you mean he cheated
on you? Did he say sorry?
He pays the bills?
And he comes home at night?
What more do you want?*

Later that night she picked the polish off
with her front teeth until the bed you shared
for seven years seemed speckled with glitter
and blood.

ii

On the drive to the hotel, you remember
the funeral you went to as a little boy,
double burial for a couple who
burned to death in their bedroom.
The wife had been visited
by her husband's lover,
a young and beautiful woman who paraded
her naked body in the couple's kitchen,
lifting her dress to expose breasts
mottled with small fleshy marks,

a back sucked and bruised, then dressed herself
and walked out of the front door.
The wife, waiting for her husband to come home,
doused herself in lighter fluid. On his arrival
she jumped on him, wrapping her legs around
his torso. The husband, surprised at her sudden urge,
carried his wife to the bedroom, where
she straddled him on their bed, held his face
against her chest and lit a match.

iii

A young man greets you in the elevator.
He smiles like he has pennies hidden in his cheeks.
You're looking at his brown shoes when he says it;
the rooms in this hotel are sweltering.
Last night in bed I swear I thought
my body was on fire.

Your Grandfather's Hands Were Brown

And your grandmother kissed each knuckle
like they were separate mountains
then circled an island into his palm
and told him what parts they would share
and what parts they would leave alone.

She wet a finger to draw where the ocean would be
on his wrist, kissed him there,
named the ocean after herself.

Your grandfather's hands were slow but urgent.
Your grandmother dreamt about his hands,
a clockwork of fingers finding places to own –

under the tongue,
collarbone,
bottom lip,
arch of foot.

Your grandmother names his fingers after seasons,
the index finger a wave of heat,
the middle finger rainfall and so on.
Some nights his thumb is the moon
nestled just under her rib.

Your grandparents often found themselves
in dark rooms, mapping out
each other's bodies,
claiming whole countries
with their mouths.

Beauty

My older sister soaps between her legs, her hair
a prayer of curls. When she was my age, she stole
the neighbour's husband, burnt his name into her skin.
For weeks she smelt of cheap perfume and dying flesh.

It's 4 a.m. and she winks at me, bending over the sink,
her small breasts bruised from sucking,
she smiles, pops her gum before saying –
boys are haram, don't ever forget that.

Some nights I hear her in her room screaming.
We play surah al baqarah to drown her out.
Anything that leaves her mouth sounds like sex.
Our mother has banned her from saying God's name.

Mermaids

Sometimes the cunt is tucked into itself,
sewn up
            like the lips of a prisoner.

After the procedure, the girl learns
how to walk again, mermaid with new legs,
soft knees buckling under new sinless body.
Daughter is synonymous with traitor, the father says.
If your mother survived it, you can.
            Cut, cut, cut.

But Mother, did you truly survive it?
The carving, the warm blade against
your inner thigh. Silencing
the devil's tongue between your legs.

On an episode of *America's Next Top Model*
the contestants huddle around Amina after her
confession, touching her arm
with concern
            for her pleasure.
Asking questions: *Can you even feel*
anything down there? The camera zooms in
on a Georgia O'Keefe painting.

Mother says
the clitoris is not a heart, you won't die
if they cut it out, just thank god
you have your arms and your legs,
some people do not even have that.

Two girls lie in bed beside each other holding mirrors
under the mouths of their skirts,
comparing wounds.

When We Last Saw Your Father

He was sitting in the hospital parking lot
in a borrowed car, counting the windows
of the building, guessing which one
was glowing with his mistake.

In Love and in War

To my daughter I will say
when the men come,
set yourself on fire.

Your Mother's First Kiss

The first boy to kiss your mother later raped women
when the war broke out. She remembers hearing this
from your uncle, then going to your bedroom and lying
down on the floor. You were at school.

Your mother was sixteen when he first kissed her.
She held her breath for so long that she blacked out.
On waking she found her dress was wet and sticking
to her stomach, half moons bitten into her thighs.

That same evening she visited a friend, a girl
who fermented wine illegally in her bedroom.
When your mother confessed *I've never been touched
like that before*, the friend laughed, mouth bloody with grapes,
then plunged a hand between your mother's legs.

Last week, she saw him driving the number 18 bus,
his cheek a swollen drumlin, a vine scar dragging itself
across his mouth. You were with her, holding a bag
of dates to your chest, heard her let out a deep moan
when she saw how much you looked like him.

Sara

i

We typed the word *clitoris* into Google
and found a numbered diagram,
then spent hours with a small mirror,
comparing.

ii

That one night when Sara
got into a car with a boy,
we all knew it was a mistake.
No one said anything when she

walked back smiling, limping.
We sat there ruined,
watching her clean the blood
from her skirt with spit.

iii

In the lunchroom, Hussein tells us
what it felt like for him. We're mesmerized.
Imagine, he says, pointing to my mouth,
pushing an entire finger

into the gap
between your front teeth.
The girl beside me shudders.

You know she begged me? Even though it hurt
she still begged me, kept whispering:
make me normal, please
make me normal, open me up.

Trying to Swim with God

Istaqfurulah

My mother says that this city is killing
all of our women. We're practising back strokes
at the local swimming pool when I think of Kadija.

The swimming instructor tells us that the longest
a human being has held their breath under water
is 22 minutes. Later, at home in the bath,
my hair swells to the surface like ink, I stay submerged
until I can no longer stand it, I think of all the things
I have allowed to slip through my fingers.

Inna lillahi Wa inna ilaihi Rajioon.

My mother says no one can fight it –
the body returning to God,
but the way she fell, face first
from that high window,
mouth full of teeth, blood –
wearing a white cotton baati,
hair untied and smoked with ounsi,
I wonder if Kadija believed
she was going to float.

ACKNOWLEDGEMENTS

For material included in this selection the following grateful acknowledgements are made: to flipped eye for poems by Malika Booker from *Breadfruit* (2007); to Peepal Tree Press for Malika Booker's poems from *Pepper Seed* (2013) and from her untitled project adapting stories from the Bible; to Jonathan Cape for poems by Sharon Olds from *Selected Poems* (2005), *One Secret Thing* (2009), *Stag's Leap* (2012) and *Odes* (2016); to flipped eye for poems by Warsan Shire from *Teaching My Mother How to Give Birth* (2011); and to Warsan Shire for her poems from *Her Blue Body* (flipped eye, 2015), a pamphlet produced at the end of her tenure as Young Poet Laureate.